HOW TO THINK LIKE AN ENTREPRENEUR

BY MICHAEL B. SHANE

NOTE TO READERS

Author Michael B. Shane
is pleased to make himself available
to share his knowledge with you and
answer your questions cost-free and
toll-free every Friday
from 9 a.m. to 1 p.m. EST
at
1-800-How-2-Think
(1-800-469-2844)

BRET PUBLISHING

BRET PUBLISHING LIMITED PARTNERSHIP
1120 Avenue of the Americas
4th Floor
New York, New York 10036

First Trade Printing: March 1994
ISBN 0-9640346-0-3

Printed in the U.S.A.

This book is dedicated to
my wife Barri, my daughters Rebecca and Emily,
and my son Theodore.

ACKNOWLEDGEMENTS

First and foremost I want to express thanks to my Mother, Edith Shane. Not only because there wouldn't even be a me without her. And not only because of her unyielding support, confidence, and encouragement. My Mother is also the first entrepreneur that I ever met. She was running her own business, a chain of beauty salons, when I was growing up, which led me into Wig Flair, my first financially successful business. This was way before the term entrepreneur was widely used, and certainly long before so many people aspired to become one.

And of course to my father, Theodore Shane. He always displayed total confidence in me and always encouraged me to do what I thought was right.

Also to Herman Kahn, the person who introduced me to the power of information. His rare combination of genius, humility, and humor is, and will remain, unparalleled. He didn't know what a hard job he was taking on when he agreed to try and make an educated man out of me in exchange for some relatively insignificant advice that I provided to his Hudson Institute.

To my sister Sandi whose enthusiasm and can-do attitude has always been helpful.

And to my brother Tom who has always been there with me to share the tough times as well as the good times. He is one of the few lawyers that I've ever met who not only understands entrepreneurs, but is one himself. And thanks to the countless others over the years who have shown so much confidence and support toward me. I only hope that in some small way I have reciprocated.

To Rollin Binzer, for helping me consolidate my thoughts on paper and for helping me write and for art directing the book. To Nils Eklund, who did the illustrations and the original painting for the cover. To Ed Sessa for his input and encouragement throughout the project. To Marc Berkowe, who assisted wherever needed and whenever asked, and whose eagerness, willingness, and energy is always uplifting. To Ethel Weinberg, who did a superb job copy editing the book. And to Stanley Debel for typesetting the book. His professionalism and responsiveness were instrumental in the book's completion.

To my wife whose support is endless and whose loving criticism is invaluable.

And last, to all those entrepreneurs who came before me and to all those who will come after, who dream that great dream of personal independence.

TABLE OF CONTENTS

INTRODUCTION

Becoming an Entrepreneur

If you are like most people in the world, you work for someone else and are dependent on others for your livelihood and security. Entrepreneurs, on the other hand, choose to think for themselves and run their own businesses for the sake of financial and personal independence.

A useful device—the Mirror Test—measures your independence quotient. When you wake up in the morning and look in your mirror, who do you see? Do you see yourself? Or do you see your boss? You have to understand that when you work for someone else you are in many ways a reflection of that person, and not of yourself. Even if your boss is the best in the world, someone you like and respect, you are still using up your life every working day, building his or her independence and fortune instead of your own. That's why the boss shows up in your mirror.

Independence is the deep-rooted motivator of all entrepreneurs. The roots of my own need for independence took hold when I was only seven. I loved sitting and talking to my father in his doctor's office. On one of these occasions I remember sitting opposite his desk while he explained what going into the hospital meant. Only this time, my father, not one of his patients, needed surgery. I perceived immediately that something in my life was

The Mirror Test.

changing, but I couldn't put my finger on exactly what it was. Many years of treatments and operations later, my father passed away. I was seventeen. It was then that I realized what the change was that I had begun to feel ten years earlier. It was a great need for emotional and financial independence. I knew it was time to think for myself.

Ultimately the key to your personal independence is in the mind. Becoming a successful entrepreneur allows you the ultimate freedom, freedom of your own thoughts. The independence of your own thinking is the only real source from which all other forms of independence flow.

Success liberates your mind. A mind free to gather information and think without unwelcome influences and constraints from others is the greatest reward an entrepreneur can receive. You can spend your time thinking about what you want to think about. Having this powerful drive for freedom of thought and independence is essential to becoming a successful entrepreneur. Everything else can be learned.

The quicker you learn, the better, of course. The simple truths you will find in this book took me over 25 years to learn—the hard way. How I wish I'd known these things when I started my first business. Hopefully, this book can speed up the learning process for you.

If you want to become independent in thought and action, you simply must cross over the line of dependence (employment) and start making efforts to control your own destiny and fortune every day. The basic tenet about independence is that you have to do it for yourself.

In today's world, independence means starting your own business. It's exhilarating and profoundly liberating to become your own boss. It's also scary. Most of us haven't the foggiest idea about how to start a new business.

Lucky for all of us, entrepreneurs are made and not born. Anyone can become one. There is no secret formula or magic touch. Prosperous entrepreneurs come in every size, shape, and personality. A million different businesses can all lead to success. There is only one common denominator: a specific pattern of entrepreneurial *thinking*.

Entrepreneurs make money with information and energy instead of making money with capital like the big guys. Entrepreneurs make money with their minds. Thinking like an entrepreneur means expanding and training your mind in specific ways that protect your independence and ensure victory.

First and foremost, an entrepreneur has the ultimate respect for new information. Information is the *basis* of everything...understanding your customers, employees, and suppliers, positioning your product or service, beating the competition, smart timing, knowledgeable decisions, operating profitably...everything.

First And Foremost
An Entrepreneur Has
The Ultimate Respect
For New Information.

If you aren't prepared to become an information junkie in your own self-interest, don't even start the process. The relentless, overriding task of an entrepreneur today is thinking about information and learning how to use it. Entrepreneurs need the drive to constantly seek out and gather new information about everything and anything that affects their business. Then they think about it, and use that information to decide and take action. Then they start the process all over again and again with new information.

Having that opportunity to gather, think about, and decide on new information is essential for success. And everyone (in the free world) has that opportunity.

CHAPTER ONE

INFORMATION
The Lifeblood of Your Business

The popular misconception is that entrepreneurs are strong-willed men and women of action. But the truth is that successful entrepreneurs are strong-willed men and women but first, of thought, and then, of action. Their primary everyday action is thinking and relentlessly seeking information to enable them to continually give their customers, employees, and suppliers what they need (require) and want (desire) and get what they need and want in return, thereby achieving the ultimate in fair play and fairness.

Information—having it and knowing how to use it—is the key to business strength. Information is the great equalizer. It has no bias. Not toward gender, race, or religion. In its simplest form, information is a single fact. It is anything you see, hear, read, touch, talk about, sniff, observe, or question. It's also any idea. It can be a word, a symbol, number, color, or comparison.

Information is the raw material for your thinking. Your mind gathers information with your five senses: smell, sight, hearing, taste, and touch. Information is anything that enters your mind. A continual flow of new information is the only way you keep a pulse on your business, set priorities, prepare for and anticipate the future. You think about it all, and use that information to make decisions and then take action.

CHAPTER ONE

No matter what business or industry you choose to become involved in, the absolute key to your success will be how well you handle information about the three fundamental areas of your business: Management, Marketing, and Money. Management, marketing, and money are like the three legs of a stool. You can't sit on a stool if one of the legs is missing.

You need to understand what information is, what information you need, where to get it, and how to use it. Nothing is more important. From day one, you've got to have all the information about every aspect of your business or you simply won't make it.

If you are going into your own business for the first time, prepare to go through a kind of human revolution as you stretch your mind and develop your skills, methods, and experience at gathering and thinking about information. Thinking about it means questioning, sorting, analyzing, dissecting, interpreting, reflecting on, organizing, and deciding upon staggering amounts of new information.

You will begin dealing with a much greater and more comprehensive scope of information than ever before. And you'll have to do it day after day, forever. It will become automatic, like brushing your teeth in the morning, except that you will do it all day, every day. The better and faster you get at gathering and thinking about new information the easier and more natural it will become. It's exercise for the mind; you'll learn to love it.

You need all three legs of the stool: Management, Marketing, and Money. If one is broken you can't sit on it.

This simple but constant mental process of gathering and thinking about new information is the only way to become knowledgeable about your business. And it's the only way to stay knowledgeable.

Knowledge is information you can use. When you find information about management, marketing, or money that you can use, a connection is made, knowledge is created. A light bulb suddenly turns on over the top of your head. It's like a kid playing the dot game who's connected enough dots to figure out the puzzle. Learning how to use different pieces of information is the nature of knowledge.

Knowledgeable decisions lead to success. They are the critical path to personal independence. So we return again to information, the source of knowledgeable and successful decisions.

Success is an ongoing process of successful decision-making. Every successful decision you make is a link in the chain of your prosperity. You have to constantly make correct decisions. And your best way of doing that is to gather all the pertinent information and think about it before you make a decision. The more and better information you have, the greater your chances of making successful decisions.

Information is the fuel for successful decisions. It powers your judgment, your plans, and your actions. Entrepreneurs have to go out and find their own fuel. But happily,

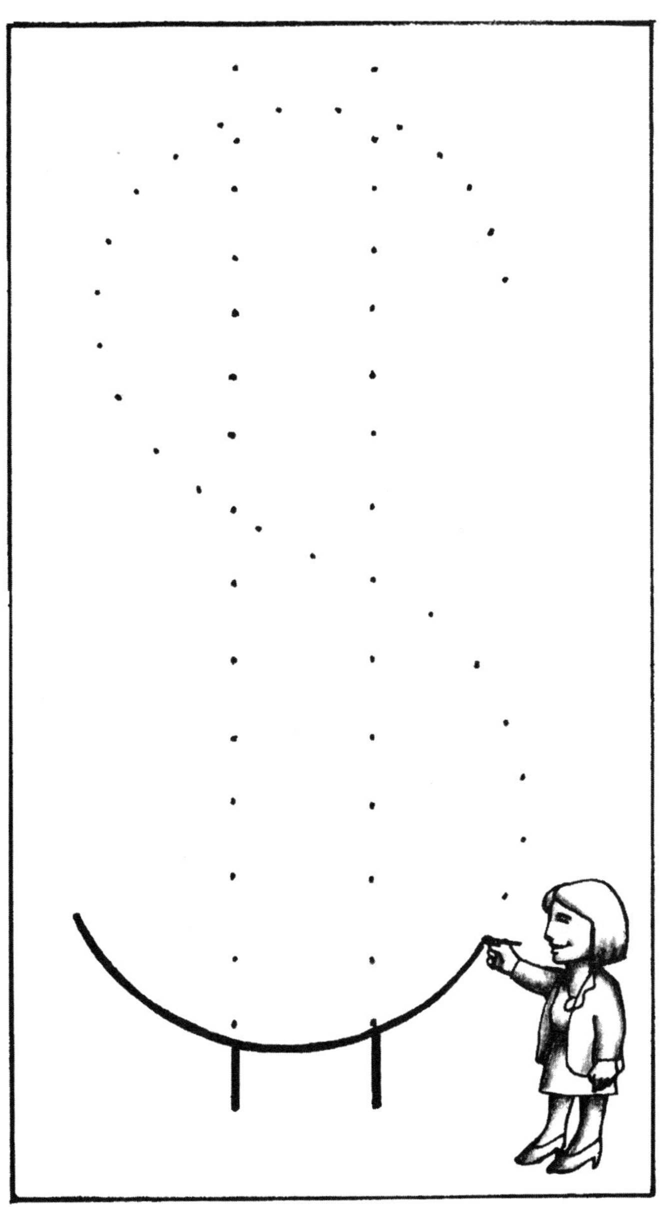

Thinking about information is like playing connect the dots.

it's everywhere. There is an abundance of information. Staggering amounts of research, statistics, reports, and opinions are available from libraries' on-line databases and countless other places. But all the information in the world is useless unless you know how to use it.

An entrepreneur uses information to start and run a successful business, and to get and keep its customers, employees, and suppliers happy. The more information you've got the more you can do. You need to know what is needed and wanted by your customers, employees, and suppliers in order to be able to anticipate and provide these things.

To a successful entrepreneur the highest order of information is that which can be:

1. Used to make money
2. Substituted for money

Using information to make money can go to the very heart of your product or service. I had watched the Japanese electronics companies for years while they were beating American electronics products because the Japanese had better prices, better features, and a reputation for excellent quality. At a seminar one day I learned that South Korea was going to be the next "Japan."

Since we were having problems getting enough computers to satisfy customer demand, it occurred to me that

To A Successful Entrepreneur
The Highest Order Of Information
Is That Which Can Be:

1. Used to make money

2. Substituted for money

South Korea might be a good place to get computers made. We were already having Leading Edge computers made in Japan, but we contacted the seven or eight largest South Korean companies and found out that one of them, Daewoo, had an IBM-compatible prototype in research and development. Although it looked like a boxcar and weighed as much as a boat anchor, we decided to do business together anyway. We contributed the design input and all the features we knew from our experience that people wanted or would soon be wanting in this category of product.

That was the Leading Edge Model D. It sold terrifically well in the United States. And it was the first IBM-compatible from South Korea. It had more features than the comparable IBM PC model for a substantially lower price, and its quality was at least as good. That one piece of information about South Korea launched our most successful computer. You never know where you'll find that one piece of information that will lead to your great success.

A good entrepreneur always finds ways to substitute information for money. For example, we once wanted to open a branch office in New York City but rents were very high and a long lease with six months to a full year's rent as a security deposit was normally required. This represented more cash than we wanted to tie up or risk at that time. And we didn't know how much space we were ultimately going to need. Then we learned about a building in a perfect location with an entirely vacant floor.

Moreover, its management was willing to rent it on a month-to-month basis, office by office, as we needed more space. This one piece of information allowed the entire venture to proceed with a minimum of cash, and to grow at its own pace.

Another example in which information substituted for money was with salespeople. When we started the Faded Glory Blue Jeans Company, our challenge was to accomplish effective national distribution without hiring a full-time sales force. When we started, it didn't make financial sense to hire and train an entire sales force. (Even if we could have afforded this vast hiring program, an entrepreneur always tries to substitute information for money.) But, the fashion nature of our products required instant national distribution or others could copy our ideas and capture the market before we did.

While digging around for a solution we uncovered information about an informal countrywide network of manufacturers' representatives. They were experienced, already had a base of clients, and they worked on straight commissions. We didn't have to pay them until the merchandise was shipped. Once again, information allowed the enterprise to go forward with speed and without a major infusion of money. Today this staffing method is sometimes referred to as outsourcing.

Many manufacturers will make products to your specifications without your having to invest in a plant or machinery. Public warehouses will store and efficiently ship your products for a relatively small fee. Bookkeeping and payroll services will provide services on a month-to-month basis for less money than your own comparable employees would cost.

Importantly, you can keep overhead down without reducing your capability, investing lots of money, or taking big risks. Today you can outsource almost anything. Today, a company that does a lot of outsourcing is sometimes referred to as a "virtual" corporation.

The faster you learn how to gather, think about, and use information, the more knowledgeable your decisions will become and the better your business will progress. It's known as cause and effect.

CHAPTER TWO

WHERE AND HOW DO YOU GET INFORMATION?

You Are Your Own CIO

Gathering information is an intelligence operation. Intelligence is having the information...and knowing what to do with it. The job of an intelligence operation like the CIA or any good detective is to constantly seek and find the information.

After intelligence officers get information, they think about it, analyze it, organize it, add the new information to the old information, and rethink it again. (A good intelligence officer or detective has a way of seeing meaning in the information that others might overlook.) Then, at some point, that information becomes the basis for making strategic plans and decisions and taking actions. Clearly, the United States government has to know anything and everything that's going on around the world. It can't operate sensibly or successfully without information and intelligence. And neither can you.

Every big company and every top executive in the world have people who constantly read mountains of material for them and pass on the information of interest. It's their intelligence system. Today some companies even have CIOs (chief information officers). But in your own business, you're the CIO.

You are your own CIO.

Information-gathering techniques are plentiful. Questions are one of the powerful tools. In school we're not taught to question. If we work for someone else, we're not taught to question. But questions are a powerful tool for learning. Train yourself to constantly ask a lot of questions. Business is a world of infinite what's and why's and how's. What does it take to make or provide the best product or service in the industry? Why isn't my product or service already the best in the industry? Why didn't the applicant for the controller's position who I wanted to hire accept the offer? Why did my top salesman sell less product last month? Why did I get less inquiries from my advertising last month? Why did my gross margin decrease last month? Why did my inventory build last month? Why didn't my cash flow increase last month? Why did two people leave the company? What could I have done better to anticipate my customers, employees, and suppliers' needs and wants?

There is no such thing as a "dumb" question. What's dumb is to refrain from asking a question. You can get more valuable information with one smart question than you can get from reading 20 textbooks.

We asked one question at Leading Edge: Will people buy a clone of the IBM PC that functions exactly the same, has more features, sells for less than one-half the price, but that doesn't have the IBM name?

The answer we got (which was different from what the

industry experts were saying at the time)—an emphatic "yes"—ignited the entire IBM clone industry. Our sales soon zoomed to over $200 million per year.

You can also learn a lot by observing people (like a detective does). A person's behavior is usually more revealing and honest than anything he or she says. (What a person doesn't say and do can be as important as what that person does say and do). For instance, you can learn a tremendous amount by watching people as they shop and compare products. Observing the action patterns and attitudes of your potential customers yields essential information.

Learn how to seek out information in all the regular places. Every industry has its traditional sources of information: trade organizations, trade shows, trade publications and magazines, business magazines (such as *Fortune, Forbes, Business Week, Inc, Success,* and *Entrepreneur*), consumer magazines (such as *Time, US News and World Report,* and *Newsweek*), newspapers (the *Sunday New York Times* Business section and the business section of your hometown newspaper, the *Wall Street Journal*), electronic bulletin boards, databases, networks like Internet and on-line information services and gateways like Compuserve, America Online, GEnie, Delphi, eWorld, Dow Jones News/retrieval, and Prodigy, the yellow pages, libraries, and CNN to name just a few.

Learn to be a channel surfer. Use your TV remote control, browse in bookstores. These are all good places to start gathering information but bad places to stop. Participating in the various events and activities of your industry is also a mandatory minimum of your information-gathering process. You have to know at least as much as everybody else in the industry. But the obvious trick is to know more.

Thousands of trade organizations are in Washington. And they are usually brimming with information. Also, the Small Business Administration (SBA) has a treasury of information about almost every industry and much of it is not widely published.

SCORE, a national organization of retired executives, works closely with the SBA and can be a good source of information. Check what programs your own state government has available. And many local colleges and universities offer courses on entrepreneurship.

If your business involves foreign trade, the United States Commerce Department in Washington has a person dedicated to coordinating business information with each country in the world.

An extension of your own conversations with others is networking. Networking is having a web of contacts with whom you share and exchange helpful information (when you network you are using information as a tradeable currency) on a regular basis—people who you talk to and connect with in business, such as other entrepreneurs, lawyers, your potential customers, employees, suppliers,

NETWORKING IS HAVING A WEB OF CONTACTS WITH WHOM YOU SHARE AND EXCHANGE HELPFUL INFORMATION (WHEN YOU NETWORK YOU ARE USING INFORMATION AS A TRADEABLE CURRENCY) ON A REGULAR BASIS.

competitors, store owners, possible mentors, accountants, and consultants.

Entrepreneurs must continually expand their circle of contacts (a major source of information). Anyone who has built a successful business will tell you it's not what you know *or* who you know that counts. *It's both.*

My first networking experience happened in the wig business. My office neighbor, Jack Stein, was also my mother's friend. Jack became my first business mentor. He was in the cosmetics business. He had a contract to train a large airline's flight attendants to improve their appearance with the proper use of cosmetics. He learned that many attendants were interested in purchasing wigs. He shared that information and made the introductions for me. I wound up selling a substantial number of wigs to those flight attendants.

Over the last 28 years many mentors have been part of my network. It is very important to evaluate each piece of information, of advice, separately. Take the information and advice and use it only if it makes sense to you. Do not follow all of any one person's advice blindly.

Everyone in your network, including you, brings what and who they know to the table for mutual exchange and benefit. Always have great respect for your network of contacts. It's like your brain trust. Keep it growing and make the deliberate effort of keeping in touch and sharing information with people on a regular basis. Never burn bridges. Information can change very fast and someone who you perceive to be an adversary can turn into an ally overnight. Your network is a primary source of information and opportunity as well. Actively keep up your network. You should touch base with everyone in your network at least every 60 days. You never ever know when or from where key pieces of information will come.

Every entrepreneur has to become a CIO and set up his or her own intelligence system. Gathering information, thinking about it, and then deciding on a course of action is the essential job in business today.

Your success will depend on doing this work very well. And even when you become big enough to have other people do it for you, no one will ever be able to use information and apply it in your business like you will. Just as no two people are exactly alike, no two people interpret information exactly the same way. Each person has a basis of information and experience that's unique.

CHAPTER THREE

What Information Do You Need?

You Must Start with a Business Plan

For starters, you need every bit of necessary information to write a business plan. A business plan is the blueprint for building your dream business. It includes an informational checklist of all the nuts and bolts that go into the three fundamental areas of every business: Management, Marketing, and Money.

First, you'll use your business plan to help you gather information and test your idea to see if you should even start your business. Second, you'll use it to get financing You must have adequate financing. If you are undercapitalized your thinking will not be clear, and your decision-making ability will therefore suffer immensely. And third, the business plan will be an ongoing operating plan.

Starting your own business is like building a house. You wouldn't start building a house without a blueprint, right? You would need to know all sorts of information first: How much lumber do I need? What kind? How many windows? How many doors? What kind of plumbing? What about permits? Similar information is included in a business plan.

Every business is a whole system. Its purpose is to make customers happy, but each element affects every other element. It's like a bowl of jello. If you touch only one

A BUSINESS PLAN
IS THE BLUEPRINT
FOR BUILDING YOUR
DREAM BUSINESS.

part, it moves everywhere. Weakness anywhere is potential weakness everywhere. That is the reality of running your own business.

That's why you need an integrated business plan. Each fundamental area of your business—management, marketing, and money—affects the others. You must break the whole down into parts and make sure that each part is healthy and fueled with the right information.

The structure of your business plan will help you test your idea, know every aspect of your business, anticipate problems, and have a handle on them from the day you start until the day you finish, no matter how small or big your business is. Your business plan should keep changing through your constant updating.

Share your business plan with key employees, outside advisors, and with anyone else you trust and think can give you good input.

If I had used a business plan as a test, I wouldn't have gone into certain businesses at all. If I had used a business plan as an operating plan, I would have been even more successful in certain other businesses.

BUSINESS PLAN OUTLINE

(The following is meant as an outline only. Refer to the many software programs and books about business plans for more specific guidance.)

Where's your blueprint?

THE ENTREPRENEUR'S SUMMARY

This section of the plan must clearly and concisely spell out the concept of the business, i.e., the product and/or service that you are going to start.

Describe the specifics and special opportunities of your concept, the uniqueness of the product or service you are offering, and why it will be attractive and pleasing to your potential customers.

Describe how you intend to reach those customers. On what special basis and/or with what unique ability do you intend to attract, satisfy, and keep customers happy? Include how these customers' needs and wants might change in the future, and how you will meet that challenge.

Describe why your business will succeed. Remember to focus on your potential customers at all times. Remember also when you're trying to define who your customers are, ask yourself who you can help, how you're going to help them, and how you're going to help them better than anyone else.

I. MANAGEMENT

1. *Entrepreneur's background and experience.* Include your own history, education, work experience, hobbies, and interests. Anything that helps to focus on your ability to understand, manage, and grow your own business and to meet the needs and wants of your proposed customers, employees, and suppliers.

2. *Personnel, administration, and organization.* Key people in your business and their experience. Organization charts. Staffing and training. Professionals, consultants, advisors, lawyers, accountants, informal or formal advisory committee, and board members.

II. MARKETING

1. *History of industry.* When and why did the industry begin? What changes has it gone through? What is the current state of the industry?

2. *Competitive analysis of market.* Trends and growth potential, competitors' profile, competitive grid (see illustration on page 77), comparison of strengths and weaknesses vis-à-vis the competition, and government regulations, if applicable.

3. *Market strategy positioning.* Strategy for product/service differentiation, pricing, quality, customer service and support, warranty policies, advertising, packaging, public relations, promotions, direct mail, etc.

4. *Target market.* Size and growth potential of your market. Who are your primary customers? How many are there? Where are they? How much money do they spend (or would they spend) on your product or service every year? What are you offering that will satisfy your customers' needs and wants better than the current competition? Or, why will it be opening up a new market?

5. *Sales force and distribution system.* How will you sell your product/service and who will sell it? Will you sell direct to the customer? Or will you sell to retail stores direct or through distributors? Will you use telemarketers? How does your product or service get to the customer?

6. *Manufacturing/servicing processes and operations.* Include labor considerations and the environmental and economic impact.

III. MONEY

1. *Financing required.* Cash flows and profit and loss statement. One year in detail plus two additional years sketched out.

2. *Risks.* What can go wrong with the plan?

3. *Worst-case scenario.* What happens if everything that can go wrong with the plan does go wrong?

You will also need information about where to get the money to begin your business (if you don't already have it). Start with friends and relatives, local investors, and other entrepreneurs. Also, approach your potential suppliers or people who can benefit from your being in business, such as a potential landlord, a parts supplier, or even your customers.

In fact, when we introduced the Leading Edge Model D, to ensure a spot in the delivery cycle and to allow us to, in the beginning, get rock-bottom prices from the manufacturer, Leading Edge retailers advanced, over the course of three years, approximately $480 million, which Leading Edge retailers sold for approximately $1 billion. (Leading Edge shipped to the retailers approximately $470 million of merchandise and approximately $10 million of product was shipped to the retailers by Daewoo as part of the purchase price of the company.)

You can also approach venture capitalists. Although they now seem much less interested in investing in start-ups, these sources are still worth pursuing (if nothing else, you will learn how they think). What friends and relatives, potential suppliers, investors, and lenders expect in return will vary vastly, depending on the particular situation, business, and industry you're involved in.

Finally, if your strength is only in management skills, you must acquire (learn or source) the marketing skills. If you possess only marketing skills, then you must acquire management skills. If you don't have either you probably won't be able to attract money.

If you've got only the money, you have to acquire the management and marketing skills before you start or there's a good chance you'll lose your money.

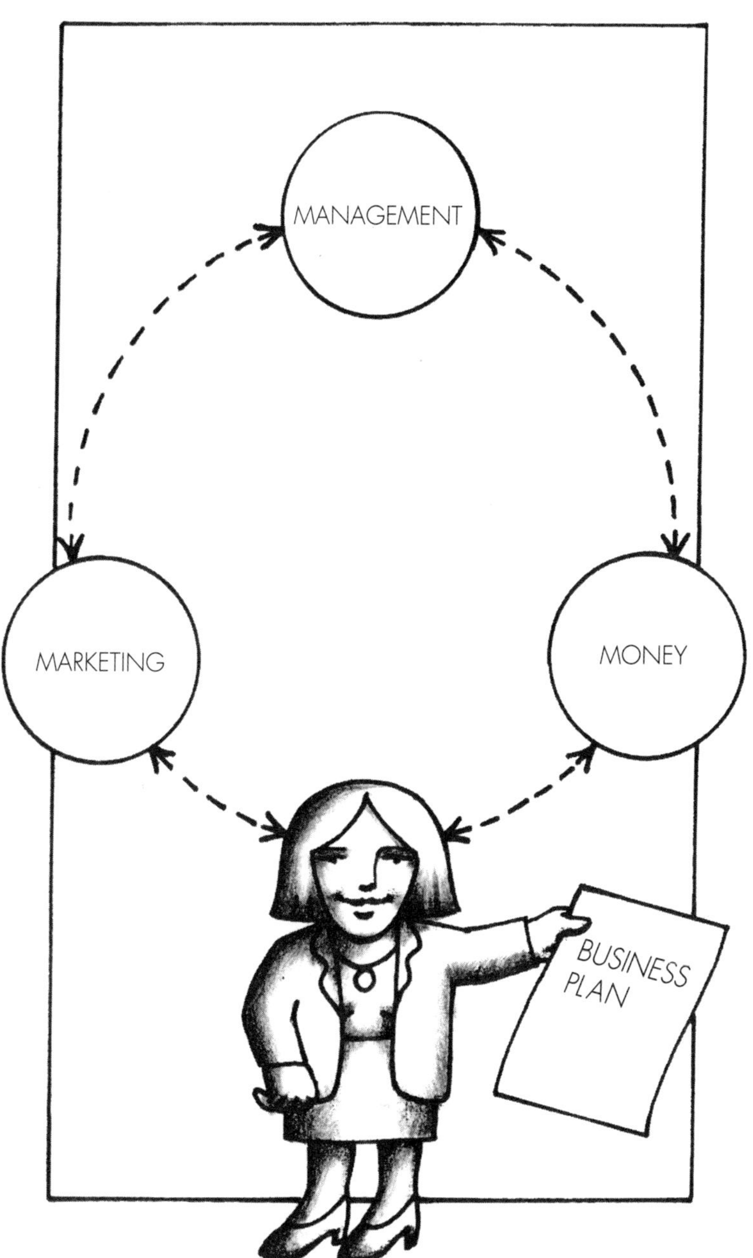

You must master the three fundamental areas of business.

CHAPTER FOUR

DECISIONS: SUPERFICIAL, GUT, AND KNOWLEDGE

A System for Making Decisions

The ultimate reason for gathering information about your customers, employees, suppliers, competitors, and the world around you is to prepare you for making decisions. Your success as an entrepreneur depends totally on using information to make correct decisions continuously.

Information is the vital fuel for decisions, but unless you use information to create knowledge all the information in the world won't necessarily lead to a successful decision.

How can you train yourself to consistently make knowledgeable, successful decisions? Use this three-part system to develop the skills of a master decision-maker. The basic principle is to: *Gather and think about as much relevant information particular to the situation as you can before making a decision.*

First think through the reason you are making a decision. Is it to solve a problem? Enhance a situation? Institute new ideas? Improve your product or service? Save money? Protect your independence?

The idea isn't to make as many decisions as you can. The idea is to make the right decisions. This system encompasses the three types of decisions: superficial, gut (or instinct), and knowledge.

SUPERFICIAL DECISIONS

In the decision hierarchy, superficial decisions are the lowest and most obvious form. Superficial decisions are just what they sound like. They are based on first impressions and outward appearances—not on a thorough examination of the issues.

A superficial decision can be likened to judging a book by its cover. It's not a reliable method. It's not based on logic. A superficial decision is usually made long before enough information is available to fully understand a situation, and based on superficiality. There's more than meets the eye in most instances. Therefore, the best decisions aren't always obvious and shouldn't be made immediately.

Superficial decisions are often wrought with prejudice, misinterpretation, or prejudgment—your own or someone else's. For example, you might make a superficial decision based on something you've read in the press, without checking any further. News articles are sometimes written by people who are unfamiliar with the subject they are writing about. Simply because something is published in a major newspaper doesn't mean it's correct. It only means that it could be correct.

The question remains, How do you stretch your knowing beyond the obvious? Beyond the superficial?

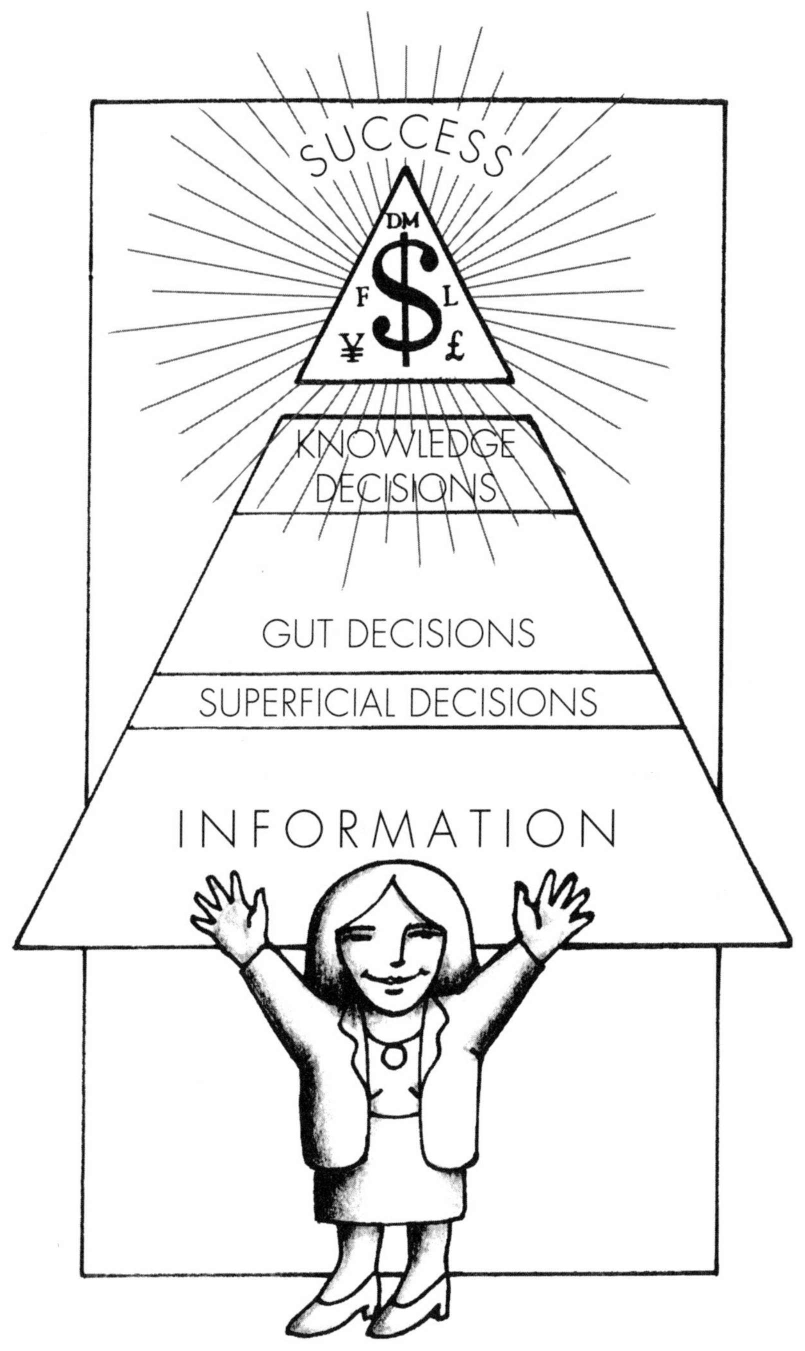

The three types of decisions.

The answer is fourfold:

1. Get more information
2. Have patience
3. Follow your instincts
4. Think

GUT DECISIONS

The second type of decision is a gut decision. Gut decisions have more credence than superficial decisions. Gut decisions are based on gathering more information and on more thinking. Gut decisions are also based on instinct, an inner sense of knowing the right thing to do, which is a difficult, if not impossible, task to explain.

When you are trying to break through competition or satisfy customers in a new way or treat people more fairly or leap to a new level in your product, service, distribution, or advertising, you need to transcend the obvious. So you keep gathering and thinking about the information. But have the courage to follow your gut instincts.

Follow your inner sense about the right direction to pursue. Consider your gut instinct to be your inner business partner. A partner that will grow as you grow and will become experienced as you do. A gut decision, supported by additional information, careful thought, and instinctive judgment, will obviously be much better than a decision based on superficial impressions alone.

Neither superficial nor gut decisions are based on logic,

and both are subject to change based on new information and additional thought.

If you are missing important information, your gut can be wrong. I had interviewed a man for the job of vice president of market research. The position was an integral part of our marketing department. Everything on the applicant's resumé, everything he told me at our first meeting, everything I learned from his references, indicated that he was highly experienced and competent for the job. My superficial judgment and my instinct told me, "He's the guy." So, I made a gut decision and we hired him.

Traveling was an important aspect of the job. The one thing he didn't tell me (and the one thing I didn't ask about) was that he was terrified of flying and therefore couldn't travel. At the time of his interview, we needed a good market research person. And we needed that person right away. It seemed as if the risk of making *no* decision was greater than the risk of making the wrong decision. So we made a gut decision, without all the information. What you don't know can hurt you.

The pitfalls of making gut decisions with missing information can be quite serious. We once entered into a long-term contract for supply of Leading Edge PCs with Mitsubishi Electric Corporation of America (MELA). The contract called for Mitsubishi to lower its prices to reflect changing "market conditions." (We anticipated that our presence in the marketplace might encourage IBM to lower its prices.) Mitsubishi was obviously very strong, committed, and capable of delivering the product on the agreed upon terms. This was a major decision. We were the first to import virtually 100% IBM-compatible computers from Japan.

As anticipated, IBM dropped its price drastically, and "market conditions" changed. But Mitsubishi could not respond quickly enough because of a complex financial interrelationship between the Japanese parent company Mitsubishi Electric Corporation (MELCO) and the U.S. subsidiary, Mitsubishi Electric America (MELA), which we had contracted with. Somehow in our negotiations we had failed to get the complete information that we were actually dealing with two different Mitsubishis, and that one would have to get permission from the other to honor the pricing provisions of our contract. Had we known this, we would have insisted that both Mitsubishis sign the contract, or we would not have started working with these companies.

Because we didn't have the information, we did start working with them, and it hurt us badly. When IBM dropped its prices we were not able to respond.

My original gut decision, to move forward with Mitsubishi, had seemed so correct at the time. They hadn't given us any information about the complex interrelationships between the "two" Mitsubishis. (In fact there are many Mitsubishis, all representing themselves with the same three-diamond logo.) We thought we were dealing with one company.

We hadn't made a knowledge-type decision. Again, we were in a time-sensitive situation. We thought it was important to be the first company to offer an IBM-compatible imported from Japan. We felt the risk of making no decision or delaying a decision on a supplier seemed greater than making the wrong decision. We were eager to get started in the PC business. We thought we had all the information we needed. We were wrong.

Obviously, the difference between a gut decision and a truly knowledgeable decision is *information and experience.*

I also made a gut-type decision with Daewoo to start importing computers (the Leading Edge Model D) from South Korea.

One day, a fax from Daewoo informed us that our prices were abruptly being raised. This increase drastically cut our gross margins without warning. And at the time, competition in the marketplace made it impossible to raise prices. Unlike the automobile business, in which prices usually go up, in the computer business they always go down.

In my opinion, Daewoo wanted to control our distribution channel, which had created great wealth for Daewoo and it started to squeeze us. (Our distribution channel represented the knowledge of how and where to market our products. There was great value in that knowledge.) Our substantially reduced gross margins created an operating loss that eventually forced the company into Chapter 11. Subsequently, Daewoo was able to buy Leading Edge out of Chapter 11 for approximately $16 million. It was worth about 20 times that much to them. Dealing with foreign corporations is especially difficult and requires a lot more investigation because the information and the rules they play by are so different. If I had had all the necessary information (which wasn't available at the one-day seminar that I attended and which I didn't investigate adequately) about Daewoo's business practices, I would have had it provide all the financing for the company. I didn't have all the information I needed. My decision wasn't a knowledge-type decision.

The great challenge for entrepreneurs is making smart, sound, knowledgeable decisions time after time.

KNOWLEDGE DECISIONS

Decisions based on knowledge are highest on the scale of success. Knowledge-type decisions are based on having all of the important information and a huge amount of experience so that you'll know exactly what information you need and what questions to ask. These decisions are also based on logic and are therefore fully explainable. When you know your decision is correct—when you don't have to question anyone else or yourself as to whether or not you made the right decision, you've made a knowledge-type decision.

Without all the necessary information, knowledge-type decisions are impossible. That's why having patience and relentlessly gathering, thinking about, analyzing, questioning, and pondering all the information is so vitally important. That's why you always have to extend yourself and make sure all the cards are on the table before you make a decision.

You must set up a system for getting all the information you need. For example, in the garment industry we were constantly under pressure to make style decisions for our Faded Glory line. Any fashion business must introduce fresh designs, but doing so is risky. We had been making gut decisions about which items to produce and the results were erratic.

We needed better information to make knowledge-type decisions. To solve the problem we developed a method for testing our new designs. We would produce a sample of new items under consideration and ship them to ten test stores. Within a few days we knew which items were and weren't selling. This data provided the information we needed to know directly from our customers. We used it to make knowledge-type decisions.

It is a misconception that entrepreneurs are supposed to sit behind a desk and make decisions all day long. Neither the speed or quantity of your decisions will lead to success. The quality of your decisions is what matters. Patience is always the key.

When you gather information, exercise patience until you get all the information you need. When you think about it, patiently try to understand the true nature of a situation instead of rushing to a conclusion. (Don't even think about making a decision until you have gone through this process.)

Remain patient until the right decision becomes apparent. Always restrain yourself from making a decision when you're emotional, frustrated, or tired. If possible, postpone decision-making until you feel sure you can reach a knowledge-type decision. You must have patience until you arrive at a solution. And until then, you have to keep adding fuel—information—and keep thinking about the solution, in order to make a good decision.

Try to make only knowledge-type decisions. Make any other decisions only when no more information is likely to become available to you or when the risk of not making the decision outweighs the risk of making the wrong decision. Many decisions you make are, for all practical purposes, irreversible and have irreversible consequences.

When you make a decision you are passing judgment on a person or a situation or both. You are passing judgment on your future. You are taking on a great deal of responsibility, because you should and will be held accountable for your decisions.

TRY TO MAKE ONLY KNOWLEDGE-TYPE DECISIONS. MAKE ANY OTHER DECISIONS ONLY WHEN NO MORE INFORMATION IS LIKELY TO BECOME AVAILABLE TO YOU OR WHEN THE RISK OF NOT MAKING THE DECISION OUTWEIGHS THE RISK OF MAKING THE WRONG DECISION.

Approach each and every decision-making with great care and respect. Ask yourself why you're making a decision at that moment. It's often better to defer decision-making than it is to make a decison if you feel it won't be a knowledge-type decision.

One of the principal reasons to become an entrepreneur is the independence to make your own decisions, at your own speed, about things that affect your life and livelihood. You need to make conscious efforts to build your decision-making skills. And most of us have to learn the art of patience.

Out of every ten hours you spend at work, maybe ten minutes will be spent actually making decisions. The rest of the time will be spent gathering the information and thinking about it. When you know you're missing some piece of information, making a decision can be disastrous. Never make snap decisions or allow an artificial deadline to pressure you into making an uninformed decision. Think patience. Knowledge-type decisions require time, information, and experience.

Follow the rules of thumb on the three types of decisions:

1. Always try to make knowledge decisions
2. Failing that, make gut decisions
3. Avoid superficial decisions like the plague

When you are solving a problem, you collect information and you think about it until you are certain that you have the right information and experience (your own or someone else's) to make a knowledge-type decision. If you don't feel that you have reached the correct decision, collect more information, ask the opinion of others who you think have the knowledge to help you, and keep thinking about the answer. Always reach out for the missing information. Go that extra informational mile before you make a decision.

The better your information gathering and the more experience you gain, the better your decisions will become.

Study your own decisions. Before you make a new decision analyze your previous decisions. Why did they work? Why did they not work? What could you have done differently? What would you do next time? What was the final outcome, including the unexpected? Always analyze your successful decisions as much as your unsuccessful ones. If you made the right decision, move on. If you made the wrong decision, correct it. You can lose all the momentum you've built up with one bad decision.

You have absolute responsibility for *all* of your decisions.

CHAPTER FIVE

Management

Using Information to Create Positive Situations as Dreamer, Manager, and Role Model

You are the dreamer and visionary. To produce the personal independence and prosperity you want, you must have a clear, powerful vision of creating a successful, profitable business and of satisfying your customers, employees, and suppliers.

You are the boss and manager. Good management is information-based. It is gathering, thinking about, exchanging, interpreting, and deciding on any and all information that affects your business and customers.

Good management uses information to create positive situations that make positive things happen. It is an invigorating process because all of your thoughts and efforts have a direct and tangible effect. Everything you do—or don't do—determines the successful outcome of your business. That's why you have to pay attention to every detail and be totally organized and thorough.

Management is handling the total information flow. Proactive management is constantly going out after all possible information about management, marketing, and money. It is the demanding job of dealing with information about a thousand and one interconnected details at the same time, calmly and clearly, without being overwhelmed.

The classic books on management technique are always pertinent, of course. Basically, their traditional, "What you do," advice consists of four elements:

1. Establish objectives
2. Make a plan
3. Execute the plan
4. Implement controls

Management, for today's entrepreneur, is using information as a creative tool for setting objectives, making plans, accomplishing goals, and establishing controls. Real creativity for an entrepreneur is creating positive situations by using information to build knowledge, direct action, generate and implement new ideas, and solve problems in positive ways. It is focusing the total flow of information toward making smart, knowledgeable decisions.

A string of successful decisions always creates positive situations as well as profits. That is the ultimate function of management.

A good entrepreneur manages by practicing, every day, the art of satisfying as many people as possible and by creating positive situations. Good managers in all realms treat their customers well. They give their customers what they want and need, and their customers respond in kind. This management principle works as well with your employees and suppliers as it does with your customers.

Good management continually gathers information about

customers, suppliers, and employees and tries to understand them so well that it can recognize and anticipate their needs.

At Faded Glory Blue Jeans, we wanted to hire an executive who was quite eager to join our company. He wanted the job, but for some reason he couldn't quite articulate, he was hesitant. The job required him to relocate to Boston. During the interview we learned that his young son was in the middle of his school year. Knowing how difficult uprooting kids is, especially in the middle of a school year, our human resources person suggested he commute until the end of his son's school year at the company's expense. He was so relieved. He himself hadn't realized how much this issue was weighing on his mind. This grateful executive soon after developed a highly profitable sportswear line for us.

Always strive to create unity by trying to put yourself in the other person's shoes, whether it is your customers, employees, or suppliers, and try to understand issues from their point of view. And of course to do that, you need all the information that they have and are using with which to think.

If you satisfy your employees' needs and wants then they should satisfy your needs and wants. It's common sense. Yet, it's uncommon practice.

To continue to build your company, everybody you deal

with must feel like they're winning. You can't afford any losers. A team effort must exist between employers and employees, and between a company and its suppliers. Team effort demands a healthy sharing and exchange of information. All involved should understand their value and feel good about their involvement. Every person in your company should feel as important and integral a part of your company as a heart is to the body. You want to constantly strive to create an atmosphere of complete unity. People who feel included and good about themselves produce good results. Ideally, you want everyone to become a salesperson for your company because they think so well of it.

A good manager is constantly gathering information, thinking about it, sharing it, making decisions with it, or taking action to create positive situations.

Ultimately, the skills you have and develop to manage both people and information will determine the level of your success. You must realize that only in working with others will you maximize your own potential and eventual success.

Here are some management tips that I've learned along the way:

The Golden Rule of Management

Management is the art of giving people (customers, employees, suppliers) what they need and want (or at

THE GOLDEN RULE
OF MANAGEMENT
Management is the art of giving
people what they need and want.
And simultaneously getting what
you need and want in return.

least giving them what they need and showing them the path to getting what they want) and simultaneously getting what you need and want in return.

Incentives

Incentives are a powerful, but underused management tool, especially when they are tied directly to people improving upon their jobs. Salespeople commonly work on a commission or incentive system but office staffers and other employees rarely do. When you give people an incentive, they do a better job. It's just human nature, pure human nature.

Incentives are a good means to create positive situations. But well-thought-out incentives require effort and energy. They also help people focus on the most important elements in their jobs. Incentives encourage people to participate to their maximum capacity. You should use incentives whenever and wherever possible.

For example, at Leading Edge Computer Products our telephone operators were very busy. They received hundreds of calls every day including many calls from potential new customers. These calls required much more attention than mere requests to speak with a certain party. The operators needed to ask and to answer questions in order to figure out the right person to direct each call to. We started giving our operators a bonus for every caller who became a customer.

We weren't asking the operators to do a salesperson's job. They were simply our first point of contact with thousands of potential new customers and it was very important for them to be helpful, efficient, take an interest in, and learn as much about the actual computers as possible. The system worked very well, everybody was happy, and we received numerous compliments about our friendly telephone operators.

Incentives needn't cost an arm and a leg. We saluted the best-performing department each month with a special luncheon.

Blind Spots

Beware (be-aware) of prejudice—your own and that of others. Nothing stops growth and blocks information flow like preconceived notions.

Never prejudge information. Make sure you have adequate evaluation time. Always question the information's source. Everyone perceives people and situations differently. Always try to get information firsthand, with your own eyes and ears. Try not to rely only on someone else.

Ego: The Big "E"

The biggest blind spot for most of us is our own ego. An arrogant, self-centered ego is the number-one enemy of success. Always challenge and question your own ego. You want to manage with information, not ego.

You can't approach situations by saying "me, me, me, I, I.

This is what I want." That sort of thinking leads to negative results. You must say, "This is what needs to be accomplished. Now, what does the other person need and want so that he or she can help me accomplish what I need and want." You must take into consideration and satisfy others' needs and wants first. Your chances of getting what you need and want decrease in direct proportion to your inability to satisfy others first. Any other way of thinking can lead to disaster.

Listen and Respect

Your most valuable management tool is the ear. Learn to use it; learn to listen. Let people finish their thoughts and try to understand what they are telling you before trying to be understood yourself. Stay very involved with your managers on a day to day basis. Listen especially to well-meaning criticism. If you don't know you have a problem you'll never be able to fix it. Respect what others are saying too. Any one of the five billion people in the world might have exactly the information, idea, or point of view that you need to hear at that very moment. You can't learn anything with your mouth open.

Slow Down and Help Speed Up

Sometimes your thinking will be going full speed ahead and the person you are dealing with is moving slowly. Slow down a little bit and work with that person to speed up a little so that you're working together to maximize the results.

Computer Power

When you start or grow a business today, a computer is an essential part of it. Computers don't think for you, but they are an indispensable tool for planning and operating. They are essential for gathering, storing, using, and communicating large amounts of information.

Don't Get Personal

Never criticize a person for a particular action that you didn't like. Criticize the particular action. Don't take things personally and don't mean them personally either. When you're upset with someone it's important to tell him or her in a very positive way exactly what you're unhappy about. Only then will you be working on the same wavelength.

Dealing with Experts

Professionals can be an excellent resource for knowledge. But respect their areas of expertise. We once had a terrific accountant whose work made it possible to borrow enough money from the bank to finance our business. He had great experience and knowledge about accounting. He had been around the fashion business for years. We foolishly followed his advice to break a deadlock over a fashion-design issue. He was dead wrong. But, he in fact had little experience with design. It was our mistake. He was a great accountant, not a great designer. When dealing with accountants, lawyers, bankers, venture capitalists, and other professionals, remember where their expertise lies. Also always try to pay them based on their performance, not on time spent.

On the other hand, even experts in their own fields are not failsafe. When the desktop computer business started to open up, industry experts said that new companies couldn't succeed against IBM. These experts failed to do adequate research. They spoke only to people at Fortune 500 companies who needed to make safe decisions, and IBM had traditionally dominated the computer business in this realm for decades. The researchers neglected to speak to mainstream America, which wanted value and didn't much care what brand name would be on a computer that had great value.

Government Agencies

Avoid treating local, state, and federal government agencies like the enemy. Oftentimes, these agencies can be helpful and many are particularly interested in being supportive to new businesses. And in today's business climate everyone is looking to entrepreneurs rather than large companies for job creation.

Even in your planning stages, identify any regulatory bodies you will be accountable to and provide them with full information about what you are doing. It's always better to get their cooperation from the very beginning.

Successful Arrogance

There is some aspect of human nature that tends to make us all nicer and more thoughtful of others before we're successful, because we want everyone's approval and we need everyone's support. Then as we become more successful and independent, we have a tendency to be less thoughtful and more arrogant. Remind yourself not to fall into this trap.

Successful people often isolate themselves, and thus cut themselves off from the information flow that helped to promote their success. The bigger your business gets, the closer you need to be to the information flow and the more involved with your customers, employees, and suppliers. Many businesses fail after a brief success simply because of arrogance.

Strength

The ability to see strengths in other people is as good as, if not better than having the strength yourself. You create positive situations by recognizing the strengths in other people and providing them with an environment in which to demonstrate and use their abilities. Helping others to develop their strengths is the greatest strength an entrepreneur can have.

Take Notes

Take good notes at meetings you attend. Write down anything you think worth remembering. You can't remember everything and you never know when information you have may come in handy. Keep folders on every topic you've covered and review them often.

Positive Growth

You can't ever stop working at anything. Management is

creating positive situations. And success is an endless stream of positive situations that cause your dream to come true. Every situation will be either positive or negative. If you are not working to make them positive, they will turn out negative. When things become negative, they stop growing. Positive energy keeps you growing.

Question Everything

Learn to question everything and everyone, including yourself and your own motivations. Try continually to question your own strengths and weaknesses. Question yourself as much as you question anything or anybody, but once you make a decision, go with it, without doubt.

Tenacity

Never doubt your own vision. An entrepreneur's most important asset is his or her own dream of emotional and financial independence. Management is how you achieve it. Don't remain discouraged by setbacks, just keep going. You will make mistakes along the way. That's how you build experience. But if you retain your vision, every single misstep will create new opportunity. And look at every negative result as an opportunity to learn and to grow. Losers never fail—they just never tried. You've got to fail once in a while to learn about winning. Don't let the daily ups and downs affect your long-term goals and your vision.

The People Problem

People are much more complex than they first appear; and they can be very manipulative in trying to rationalize what they want and why they want it. People will show you what they want you to see. It's part of your job to understand things as they are. What you don't know can hurt you. Never underestimate a person's ability to undercut your best interests for his or her own gain.

During the course of your business dealings you'll learn much about human nature. Your experience will teach you to always keep your eyes open. Once, when I was a fledgling in business, I learned that my partner had been taking kickbacks from a supplier. In another of my business ventures, the controller was a close friend of mine—I thought—until I received a strange phone call from a foreign car dealer. He told me the parts for my car were going to cost more than the price that had been quoted. The only trouble was, I didn't own a foreign car. The controller had been using company funds to foot the bill for what I believed to be his car.

You've got to learn to watch out for all the pitfalls in business, including human foibles. Remember, all corporations, no matter what their size, are run by individual people. Money is a powerful influence and motivator. Nonetheless, always give people the benefit of the doubt. Believe and trust in people, but don't be disappointed if you occasionally make a wrong call.

Choosing a Person, Not Just Filling a Position

Sometimes you meet a person and are so impressed with the person that you decide you want to hire him or her and then you find the right position for that person. People are very adaptable and able to learn new skills.

People Rise to the Occasion

Some people may seem timid or weak or limited and, on the surface, incapable of performing a certain function. It's important to give people the opportunity to excel. Your having confidence that they can do the job can be all the inspiration they need to rise both to the occasion and to your level of expectations.

Calm Your Upset

If you are upset with someone, explain the reason for your distress to that person (after you've given yourself a reasonable cooling-down period). Discuss the problem and begin to resolve it by finding a way to turn it into a positive situation. Don't speak from anger. That will only tend to escalate the negative and make the situation worse.

Know Thyself

Try to understand yourself for the sake of your own success. Be honest with yourself. Constantly reevaluate your own strengths and weaknesses. Know what you are good at and where you need additional consultants or staff to help.

Don't Be Too Busy

It's not how busy you are that counts, it's how much you

KNOW THYSELF.
TRY TO UNDERSTAND YOURSELF
FOR THE SAKE OF YOUR OWN SUCCESS.
BE HONEST WITH YOURSELF.
CONSTANTLY REEVALUATE YOUR OWN
STRENGTHS AND WEAKNESSES.

accomplish. Always take time to think about what you are doing and accomplishing.

Be Specific

It is essential that people know exactly what to expect in a job and also to know specifically what you expect of them. Constantly get feedback based on the implementation of your plan and reestablish the objectives. Train people to do their own jobs and share with them the ideas and direction of your company. Also, always give people credit for their ideas. Some entrepreneurs don't give others reasonable credit for their ideas. They tend to adopt the idea as if it were their own, or within a week they convince themselves they would have thought of it anyway. The source of a good idea is totally inconsequential.

They're All Your Decisions

Your business success depends on a continuous flow of successful decisions, so a knowledgeable management system requires that you understand the informational basis of all decisions, especially if someone else makes them. When you delegate decision-making authority to an employee, do it within a defined realm of that employee's understanding and knowledge. And be sure that you understand what in fact their realm and understanding is (i.e., sales, purchasing, packaging). Those who have decision-making powers should inform you not only of the decisions themselves, but also of the way the decisions were arrived at. You need all that information, not to check up on people, but to maintain your perspective. Remember, each decision affects the others.

Many Roads to Success

When making a decision, it is important to know what's been done before, i.e., the conventional thinking, history, and traditions of business, so to speak. But unless something is illegal, immoral, or fattening, always be prepared to try what you think will work. Many roads lead to successful decisions and in many instances they are the ones that haven't been traveled on before.

All Eyes Are on You

When you're the boss it's important to realize that people take what you say and do very seriously. The power of your actions and words have terrific influence. Like it or not, all eyes are always on the boss. Your pride, work ethic, enthusiasm, every word, every action, reaction, mood swing, attitude shift, determination, forge-ahead spirit, equivocation, or courage in the face of challenge affect everyone. You are the role model. People will copy you and evaluate you.

Your employees and your business are a reflection of you. You have a great responsibility.

CHAPTER SIX

NEGOTIATING

Establishing the Greatest Degree of Cooperation

In business, you are continually negotiating with everyone—your customers, your employees, and your suppliers—you come in contact with. Business is, in a sense, one continual negotiation.

The dictionary defines negotiation as, "To confer with another in order to come to terms." Contrary to popular belief, negotiating doesn't mean beating the other guy. Negotiating means sharing information to find ways to cooperate so that everyone gets what they need and want.

If you have to rely on a person or another company or a supplier on a regular basis, you want to make a deal that gives you the best advantage possible but that also gives the other party what they need as well. Otherwise they're not going to perform, and you're not going to be happy. Business should be a game, a game in which everybody wins. And that's how you keep your business growing.

When your objective is to give other people what they need and want, you are forced to look at situations from their point of view. And the essence of positive negotiation is having information about what the other party needs or wants, and trying to give it to them. Every positive negotiation creates an alliance to help build your dream.

The outcome of a perfect negotiation is that everybody wins.

We were negotiating with C. Itoh (now called Itochu), a large Japanese trading company, to become an exclusive distributor for two of its new printers (a daisy wheel type and a dot matrix). The company indicated it wanted to proceed with the agreement, but somehow it kept postponing the final go-ahead.

When a firm commitment was finally made, we couldn't begin buying the printers for six months, which meant that we would miss getting a six-month jump on the market. My instinct was that something was being left unsaid. I finally asked directly if there was some factor that we were unaware of.

The company was slightly embarrassed, but the reason for the time restriction was that Itoh had 1,000 older-model printers sitting in an American warehouse. The home office in Japan insisted that the older printers be sold before allowing the new ones to be shipped. And six months was the time the company estimated this would take. We knew that with our distribution system we could sell the printers much sooner. So *we* made it a condition of the exclusive distribution agreement that *we* purchase the old printers.

We signed the agreement, sold the old printers within 30 days, and within six months had sold a large number of the new printers. We were well on our way to building what turned out to be a $50 million printer distribution company. In fact we began selling so many of these printers to Apple dealers that Apple asked C. Itoh to sell the printers under the Apple label. In addition, C. Itoh was interested in direct access to the market. They approached us to buy our printer business. Together we negotiated a fair price and we sold C. Itoh the printer business. The timing worked out well for us because we were about to introduce our first Leading Edge PC.

You negotiate whenever you do business with anyone. But most people won't tell you what they want. You have to ask. It's usually a good idea to give them information first, such as what you are looking for or what task you are trying to accomplish. Share as much information as you can but don't give away competitive information. Then you ask questions: Would you like to work with our company? Can you do the job? To become a supplier of our company, what would you like in return? The only way to establish trust and a basis for working together is with open, honest, and direct questions, and information sharing.

Here are some no-fail negotiating tips:

Face to Face

Nothing replaces eye-to-eye negotiations.

Your Place or Mine

Negotiate wherever the other person feels comfortable, preferably on his or her own turf. By giving people home-court advantage they'll feel more comfortable, and you'll see their environment, which will help you understand them.

Alternative Approaches

There are two ways to negotiate. Begin by stating your exact position and don't budge, or start by asking for more than you expect and compromise.

The Winds of Change

Sometimes your proposal is totally rejected. You can make the very same proposal the following day and it will be accepted. Perhaps it was the way you presented your proposal, or the way you said it. Sometimes they just hear it differently. When you make the same proposal a day later, they might even ask why you hadn't mentioned the proposal earlier. Sometimes they may just perceive the situation differently or sometimes their situation may have actually changed. Always try to leave room or provide for a follow-up meeting should you need it. At the very least, keep the lines of communication open.

The Bottom Line

Don't accept less than what you need and what will make you comfortable. If you back off, you'll probably be very unhappy. You'll do a disservice to yourself and the person you're negotiating with.

Who to Negotiate With

Always try to negotiate with the ultimate decision-maker. It is this person's thinking that you need to have the most information about and understand. Whenever you negotiate with anyone other than the ultimate decision-maker information or its correct interpretation always seems to get lost in the translation. It's like the old telephone game you played when you were a kid.

Learn to Take Yes for an Answer

Sometimes you reach a certain point in the negotiation process (sometimes it's almost immediately) that you're getting what you want. Then you get so carried away with your power that your original goals are forgotten and you turn greedy. You get so caught up in the negotiation that you lose sight of what you were trying to accomplish. Use your negotiating strength to close a deal when your objectives are satisfied. Listen very carefully. Learn to say, "Yes, thank you. It's a deal." Learn to take "yes" for an answer.

Be Patient and Never Say No

Never be afraid to say you are thinking about something or "studying it," as Japanese businesspeople say. They never say "No." They can literally keep situations going for years until they get what they want because they understand very well how fast information and circumstances can change, and they might get what they want. Be patient. Patience is a critical factor in negotiations.

The Impasse and the Power of Dialogue

When you're at an impasse during a negotiation, take a little breathing time, maybe an hour, a day, or even a week or a month. Don't be concerned about who makes the next move. Get together again and share more information. That's how you break a deadlock. Dialogue can break an impasse. Just keep talking. Try to keep thinking about the situation in a different and more positive way. Think it through. Think about what you really mean. Try to be clearer. Ask the other person what they need, what their problem with the situation is. Ask again, and they may give you a different answer. An important element of negotiating is to refrain from placing unimportant self-imposed deadlines on anything. Don't ask anyone to rush an important decision. Sometimes negotiations can go on for months or even years until both sides are satisfied they'll both be winning.

Greed

You don't need to milk every penny out of one particular opportunity. For true entrepreneurs, opportunities are limitless. Don't be greedy with others and don't let others be greedy with you.

Persistence

Keep your goal in mind at all times. And work every possibility to reach that goal. If you can't go through the wall go over it or around it. Persistence will help you overcome obstacles to reach the perfect negotiation—a win-win situation.

CHAPTER SEVEN

Stress, Risk, and Luck

Information Is the Common Denominator

Stress and risk are usually consequences of insufficient or missing information. Stress is one of the downsides that results from not knowing everything, or at least, from not knowing enough. Stress results when you are unable to predict, control, and find ways out of a frustrating situation.

Often, information you don't know can hurt and stress you out. I certainly discovered this in my first venture, a successful wig business. We were shipping wigs from Hong Kong to the West Coast by boat, the conventional low-cost way of shipping at the time. My heart sank when I read a newspaper article warning about an impending dock workers strike. If the workers had gone on strike, our wigs could have been stuck indefinitely on the docks of San Francisco—a possibility that literally could have put us out of business.

I was in the wig business. It had never occurred to me that I needed to keep up with information about the dock workers union! Needless to say, I suffered through three stressful days until the dock strike was called off. From that day on we took *all* the issues into account before we made transportation (and other) decisions.

What you don't know can stress you out!

The main prescription for stress relief is information. Because having the right information about a situation makes it more understandable and predictable. Armed with enough information about a situation, you can think, decide, and then take action that puts you back in control. What's more, having enough information about a situation dispels frustration by enabling you to develop alternative scenarios.

Information gathering is the best way to eliminate the stress and frustration of being unable to take control of a situation. Always ask yourself: What information do I need to solve this problem or to find an alternative?

The more information you have, the more time you spend thinking about and interpreting that information before making any decision. And the more complete the information, the less risk. Consider the example of the blindfolded lady who's walking straight toward a cliff. She seems to be at risk. But if she knows that the cliff is exactly three steps in front of her, she'd be safe (as long as she could count).

When we introduced the first IBM-compatible computer from Japan, the conventional wisdom was that the business risks were enormous if not insurmountable. The experts declared that no one could compete against IBM. However, the experts were talking to managers in big corporations who were already buying IBM PCs because that route was a safe decision. They weren't talking to the

Information eliminates risk.

small businesspeople and entrepreneurs who would buy IBM-compatibles if the price were right...and these people didn't care about the perceived safety of the IBM brand.

Our company had conflicting information because we had spoken to hundreds of our printer customers. They told us that if we could provide a computer with a better price, equal features, and comparable service to that of an IBM, we would create a sensation. We knew that our potential marketing success was a sure thing because we were getting our information from entrepreneurs and small businesspeople—the very people that we knew would buy our computer.

If you make correct decisions without the necessary information, you're lucky. You may get lucky from time to time, but you should never count on it.

CHAPTER EIGHT

MARKETING

Positioning for Success

Marketing includes information about packaging, advertising, sales, sales promotion, communications, distribution, and even manufacturing.

To be a marketing success you need the right positioning. Positioning is the advantages that you promise to your customers that your product or service enjoys in the marketplace (versus the competition) and how you present (explain) and communicate those advantages to them.

Good positioning is the information about the value you're giving your customers, i.e., the proper combination of price, features, service, and quality. Is your offering better, faster, and cheaper? More reliable? Does it use newer technology? Classic design? More fun? Brighter colors? Latest fashion? Great warranty? Fresher tasting? Waterproof? Faster? Homemade? In other words, what's the advantage? You *must* establish a position of distinct advantage and value for your product or service.

Positioning is information-based. You can't possibly position your product without the necessary information about your customers' needs, wants, and desires. Compare that information with every hard fact about what the competitors are currently offering your customers. Armed with that knowledge you can find a strategy to beat your competitors. That's positioning.

Learn to make a competitive grid, or a formal way of comparing your product or service with the competition. It is simply a way to gather information and to graph the features, benefits, and cost of what you offer versus what the competition offers. The grid helps you see and evaluate the most compelling positioning.

What positioning will make the greatest number of people want to buy your product or service over the competition? That is always the key question.

To research that question, gather all available information about your customers. Who are they? Where are they? What are their wants, habits, preferences, and desires? How much do they spend? With who? How often do they buy your product or service?

Conduct the same research about your competitors. What are their strengths, weaknesses, features, benefits? What kind of distribution, pricing, service, guarantees, etc. do they offer? How loyal are their customers?

Gather important information about the marketplace itself. Is it an existing market or is it an emerging market? Each requires different strategies.

Emerging markets are in development, like personal computers were in the 1980s. Or like biotechnology is today. You are working first, to create a need or desire and second, to fill it. As information spreads (and you help

Competitive Grid

BRAND	FEATURES					PRICE
	HARD DRIVE	EXTRA MEMORY	WORD PROCESSING SOFTWARE	MONITOR	HARD DRIVE	
IBM	X			X	X	$3,365
BRAND•X	X				X	$3,125
BRAND•Y	X			X		$2,795
BRAND•Z	X	X				$2,495
US	X	X	X	X	X	$1,995

Learn to use a competitive grid. If you want to hit a grand slam, always position your product to give your customers something they can't afford not to buy.

spread it) about a new idea, product, or service the emerging market grows. Sometimes it explodes. You help to develop an awareness in the market as well as to sell your own product. Holding and increasing your market share (your percentage of the total market) in an emerging market is the challenge. Positioning is everything.

Existing, or mature, markets are those for products such as cars, soap, and groceries, for example. When starting a new business in an existing market, you immediately face tough, established competition. The market may grow with a population increase, but it won't expand from new awareness. Basically, your customers must be won over from your competition. The only way you can do this is with positioning.

In 1984 we introduced the Leading Edge Computer with huge success because it was positioned so well. IBM's Personal Computer was the standard then and it solidly dominated the market. We went head-to-head against IBM by offering a product with the right positioning.

We offered an IBM-compatible (clone) for substantially less money (IBM was incredibly overpriced because it had no real competitors) that also had more features, was of equally good quality, plus we offered one of the industry's first 800 numbers for service and support lines. We were like David fighting Goliath. Our positioning was irresistible. The PCs virtually flew out of the stores.

Nothing is so important as positioning yourself with a distinct advantage.

Nothing will ever affect your sales more than correct positioning. It's your customers' "reason to buy." (It took IBM much too long to do, but the company has become much more competitive.)

Marketing includes the job of making absolutely sure that anything and everything you do fosters and reinforces that positioning in your customers' minds and experience. "Everything" is the operative word. It's very easy to get carried away with some wonderful idea that doesn't have a darn thing to do with your positioning. Never let yourself be drawn into any promotion, product change, or advertising because it's clever, breathtaking, or trendy. Always ask yourself: Does this message and imagery present and communicate information that reinforces my positioning? (A new technology, or innovation. A better price, more features, better quality, and/or support.) If the answer is no, or even maybe, don't get involved. You're wasting your money. The most common marketing mistake is to forget to remember your positioning.

Your positioning should be embodied and clearly evident in *everything* your customers see or hear about your product—in the product or service itself, the name of your product or service, your trademark, all packaging, stationery, business cards, corporate and product brochures, direct mail pieces, product specification sheets, point-of-purchase displays, trade show displays, holiday greeting cards, forms, flyers, hang-tags, advertising, promotions, decor, signs, billboards, newsletters, videos, sales training,

NOTHING WILL EVER
IMPACT YOUR SALES MORE
THAN POSITIONING.
IT'S YOUR CUSTOMERS'
"REASON TO BUY."

press kits, and any form of communications including how your telephones are answered.

The same rule applies to your distribution chain: telemarketers, salespeople, manufacturers' representatives, sales agents, wholesalers, store managers, etc. Make sure that everyone conveys the same message. Positioning *is* your product or service in the world of marketing.

You may have to vary your positioning slightly depending on the region of the country or the actual country you are marketing in. (For example, in many countries of the world the steering wheel is on the right side of the car.)

You have an absolute duty to your customers to leave no stone unturned gathering the information about and understanding what your competition is offering. We once developed a new piece of software because we felt that no product on the market was fulfilling the customers' needs. We bought every package on the market that performed in a remotely similar fashion. We made sure our software included all the already existing useful features, then we added many new features, test-marketed the product to be sure we hadn't missed anything that the customers wanted, sold the product for less than any of the others, and gave better support. The new software was a whopping success. Gather the necessary information to beat the competition in every area and then give your customers even more.

The number-one reason why good products fail is bad positioning. If you want to hit a grand slam, always position your product to give your customers something they can't afford *not* to buy. When you find the right combination of price, features, and quality, people will automatically like, need, want, and buy your product or service. Do not go beyond the test-marketing phase with your product or service until you have perfected your positioning. Continue to gather information from your customers and competitors even after you've launched your business and always keep improving your positioning.

CHAPTER NINE

TOTAL CONTROL

The Entrepreneur's Challenge

From the very first day you start your business, you must learn to control your ego. There is one person, and one person only, in control of your business—the customer.

When people talk about entrepreneurs they often refer to them as "control freaks." But as an entrepreneur, the only control you should ever seek is control of information about what your customers want and need—and control of your own efforts to serve those customers.

Entrepreneurs are said to be fanatical, obsessive, compulsive, and driven. And well they should be when it comes to gathering information and making decisions to satisfy and serve the customer.

The customer is your source of success, security, and independence. You must commit yourself to your customers above all else.

The customer is the main character in your dream of independence and prosperity. Like the saying "behind every successful person there is a supportive spouse" goes—well, behind every successful entrepreneur there are happy customers.

Learn to control your own ego. Bonk it.

The customer is your driving force in business. Your primary thought and goal is to satisfy the customer. Nothing else you do matters if your customers aren't happy.

You build your business around your customers because without them, there is no hope for success. Of all the information that you must continually gather, think about, and use, the most vital to your dream is the information that helps you understand what your customer needs and wants.

If you give customers what they need and want, they will give you what you need and want, i.e., profits and success. And then you'll gain independence.

The concept seems almost too simple. But it's the most important part of your life as an entrepreneur. If you look closely at any business that's failing, odds are that it has somehow lost touch with the customer.

When I was in the blue jeans business, we had ten or twelve people in the shipping department packing up merchandise and sending it out to our customers as fast as possible every day. But when a call from a customer requested that an exceedingly large order be shipped that same day, the entire management staff rolled up its sleeves and started packing boxes to meet the request.

No time is better spent than observing, listening to, and talking with your customers. Your primary responsibility is

Behind Every
Successful Entrepreneur
There Are
Happy Customers.

to the customers. You are a channel for any and all information that's available in the world that benefits your customer. Remind yourself every day: you can only serve your customers by knowing them well. You've got to give customers what they need and what they want. Nothing is better for your business than satisfied customers. They tell other people, and you get more customers. Word of mouth is still the most important advertising tool in the world.

No matter how successful entrepreneurs become, they must continue to bend over backward to satisfy their customers. They must not only be aware of their customers' needs and wants, they must anticipate them. In 1987 at Leading Edge Products, Inc., our information gathering operation revealed that the era of electronic information services and gateways was upon us.

We anticipated that as people became aware of the tremendous potential possibilities, such as electronic (E) mail and instant access to huge amounts of information through personal computers, these information services would become increasingly more popular. We also knew the price of modems and electronic services themselves would come down as more information became available through them.

We were the first personal computer company to offer a modem with our personal computer as standard equipment. We also included a free introductory offer to the electronics services themselves.

Surrender your ego to your customers.

If you want to succeed, surrender your ego to your customers. This will help put you on your road to success. The key to *staying* financially successful is to remain as responsive to your customers as you were before you achieved financial success. Remember, you take orders from your customers in more ways than one.

CHAPTER TEN

YOUR COMPETITION
They're Always After Your Customers

Competition is always one of your best sources of information—both before you start your business and on an ongoing basis. If you're just starting up a business, your competition has existed longer than yours, and thus may have spent more time than you have collecting information about your current and potential customers.

Your competitors are a valuable benchmark against which you should check your own information. And if they're smart, they'll use you the same way. Are their customers happier than yours? Are you taking customers from them, or are they taking customers from you? What are they offering that you are not? What can you offer that they are not?

To help decide whether or not to start your business, gather information about all your potential competitors. Compare their products or services and make sure that you will have a competitive advantage. Perhaps you will offer a better product, a better price, better quality, or you will fill a market niche that they don't.

And once you are established, continue to monitor yourself against your competitors. You shouldn't blindly copy them or use them as a foolproof model, but at the very minimum, you should know everything that they know.

You can also use your competition as a guide to monitor the way they have used certain information. If they've done it better, you can adapt their method to your own product.

In all the businesses in which I've been involved, telemarketers spoke to customers. Not only did they sell products or services. But they also gathered competitive information. They constantly monitored the market to make sure we maintained the best positioning.

Telemarketers can get information on what customers may want and on what your competitors are offering. They can find out what your competitors may be offering in the future. Even if you have just three telemarketers each day speaking to customers in approximately 17 states each, you'll get nationwide coverage. They can literally give you daily input (in addition to sales) from hundreds of national customers. Armed with this knowledge, you'll have plenty of ammunition with which to improve your product or services.

Always maintain a competitive grid and have a system in place to continually update information about your competition. Some big companies have their employees get information by shopping their competitors.

They will also hire people to scour trade journals and the general press to keep up with information about their competition. (Competitive information is so important that some companies have been said to secretly bug competitors' hotel and conference rooms.)

The competition is always looking over your shoulder.

The competition is always after your customers. That's the nature of competition. When you lose to the competition you're putting your independence in jeopardy. Whenever you beat the competition, you are securing your success and independence.

As long as you are constantly gathering information and striving to create positive situations for your customers, employees, and suppliers you will be making it very difficult for your competitors to succeed.

THE COMPETITION IS ALWAYS AFTER YOUR CUSTOMERS.

CHAPTER ELEVEN

CHANGE

Turning on a Dime

Because of the abundance of available information and the speed with which technology can move it, today more than ever before, nothing is more certain than change. Especially in the world of business. New products are constantly entering the marketplace. New manufacturing and service technologies are appearing daily. Most people resist change. But to be a successful entrepreneur you must not only welcome change, you must also make it your ally.

To accomplish this, relentlessly gather information and knowledge about your industry and related industries. This will enable you to anticipate the future. Keep well informed so you have time to think clearly about and act on changes that might be forthcoming, instead of reacting too late, i.e., after they occur.

In 1982, we were the largest distributor of a national brand of floppy disks. The manufacturer couldn't supply us with all we could sell. From our constant information gathering in the market, it became clear to us that demand for floppy disks was going to skyrocket and that brand recognition and loyalty were minimal. The floppy disk itself was a very "plain vanilla," or generic-type, product. So rather than simply looking for an additional supplier of branded diskettes for us to distribute, we quickly came out with our own line of "branded" diskettes, which we called Elephant Memory Systems. Back then floppy disks were pretty much packaged like fan belts. So we had bright yellow and orange packages along with Elephant posters, stickers, and big Elephant head point-of-purchase displays.

Our diskettes jumped off the shelves. The product was an instant and huge success. Two years later we sold the Elephant Memory Systems division for millions of dollars.

Always use information to change for the better. Always strive to improve your situation. Look for new ways to reach your goal of emotional and financial independence. Ask yourself every day, what can I change to make things better? What can I change to make my customers happier? Where can I get new information to help me generate new and better ideas? Take the concept of constant improvement to heart. Even if something is working perfectly, ask how it can be made better. Without change there is no growth.

Always be prepared to change and turn on a dime.

CHAPTER TWELVE

SHORT-TERM AND LONG-TERM PLANNING

Cause and Effect

When you gather and think about information, it's important to think about how your plan of action will affect your business in both the short and long terms.

The basic principles of short- and long-term planning:

- For changes you want to happen tomorrow, or three years from tomorrow, you must make plans, gather information, and take action (immediately—if necessary) to implement those plans.

- Think and plan for the long term, and base your short-term actions on whatever needs to be accomplished to assure that your long-term plans will happen. Don't take any short-term action that will adversely affect long-term plans.

Every action you take will have both an immediate effect and a longer-term effect. You must consider both effects for each decision you make.

For example, before you commit to making any expenditures, consider the daily checkbook balance as well as where you want to be financially in three years. Your future plans depend on your thoughts and actions in the present. If your dreams for the future are merely

YOUR FUTURE PLANS
DEPEND ON YOUR THOUGHTS
AND ACTIONS IN
THE PRESENT.

hopes without a plan, then your actions will be based on nothing but short-term thinking. You must have an action plan for today in order to achieve your dreams tomorrow.

Operating without an action plan can be like paddling upstream. You can row, row, row all day long and still be in the same place as you started when the day has ended.

You need an action plan for each fundamental aspect of your business: management, marketing, and money. Without a master plan you'll be managing by the seat of your pants and hoping for the best. Let the plan help guide your decisions.

Let's say, for instance, that you have customer demand and need to increase your production of blue jeans by 20% per month. You have to plan for the supply of extra fabric, thread, and zippers to arrive at the proper time. You have to make sure that you have enough people, equipment, and manufacturing capacity. You may also have new cash requirements. Every detail has to be planned for. You can't leave anything to chance.

A good long-term plan often requires a short-term sacrifice, which is necessary to prepare for. The Cause and Effect Chart on the next page demonstrates:

Let's say, hypothetically, that you are selling 100,000 pairs of jeans per month. Your customers tell you (market research) that by reducing your prices 20% you'll signifi-

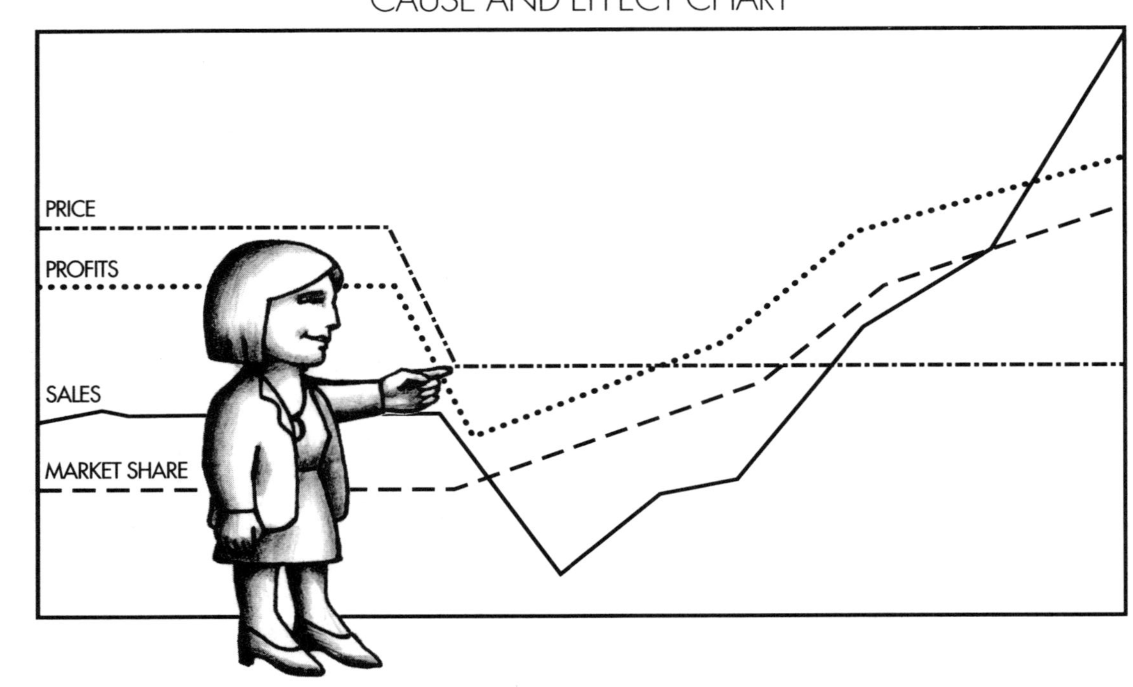
CAUSE AND EFFECT CHART
PRICE
PROFITS
SALES
MARKET SHARE

cantly expand your distribution base, the number of customers that will need or want your product.

Cause: 20% price cut.

Short-term effect: Dramatic 20% drop in gross sales receipts. This might even cost you some short-term profit.

Long-term effect: Big potential increase in gross sales receipts, market share (a lot more happy customers), and profits because you can get better prices based on volume buying. (Sometimes you can get better pricing immediately if you share the information about your long-term plan with your suppliers.)

Long-term planning is like deciding to grow a tree. First you must plant the seed to cause the tree to grow; then you must constantly nurture it. The tree will grow over time.

First you decide what the desired effect should be. Then you cause certain things to happen in order to achieve the effect. The distance between the two is the time it will take to achieve your goal.

Update your long-term plan as necessary. As your plan beomes reality, have at least one new long-term goal or objective in mind. For example, we planned to add a complementary line of sweaters to the Faded Glory Blue Jean Company. When that started to become a reality, we started planning to introduce a line of outerwear.

The key to both short- and long-term planning is to continually focus on accomplishing the original idea of giving your customers what they need and want in both the short and long terms.

CHAPTER THIRTEEN

MONEY

Information, Cash Flow, Overhead, and Profit

Contrary to popular belief, businesses don't revolve around money. They revolve around information.

You'll make money if you have the information about what your customers, employees, and suppliers need and want and if you give it to them.

Money is a by-product of information. Information directly affects everything about money—how to make it, how to raise it, how to use it, how to keep it, and how to use information to replace the need for money—and that's why it's essential to learn how information and money relate.

Basically, you use information (about what your customers need, your competition, and your product or service) to make money. You can also use information to reduce the need for money in your business operations. And most definitely, an entrepreneur uses information to find and raise the seed money for his or her new business.

Most people never really think about money except in the most static terms, or in some passive way, such as through balancing their checkbooks, filling out tax returns, or accumulating money in the bank. Start thinking about money in motion.

CHAPTER THIRTEEN

Entrepreneurs should view money as a great river of fortune rushing around them every day. People are always spending money on *something*. That's why entrepreneurs can succeed.

The best way to dip into this vast flow of cash is by having the information about and offering people a product or a service that they need or want. Something that's better, less expensive, more useful, or more unique than whatever they currently buy. When cash moves from a customer's pocket into your business, that's money in motion. That's positive cash flow.

When you pay the rent or a phone bill, that's also money in motion. That's negative cash flow. It's overhead, the black hole of business. (You should only spend money on overhead to accomplish your original idea of giving your customers what they need and want. A fancy office has absolutely nothing to do with satisfying your customer.)

Nothing in this world will so affect your independence as maintaining profits and a positive cash flow.

You can start with only $1,000 and become rich if you can maintain profits and a positive cash flow and persist. You can start with a million dollars and lose it in short order with a negative cash flow.

To maintain a positive cash flow you'll need information about the past, present, and future. Thinking about

Think of money as a great river of fortune flowing around you all the time.

money in motion demands information about cash flowing in and out of your company over given periods of time. The amount of money sitting in your bank account at a particular moment is not critical. (In fact, having too much cash can make you careless and not challenge you to think hard enough about using information to reduce the need for money. Need is the mother of invention.) Keeping the amount of money flowing into your company every month greater than the amount of money flowing out is supercritical.

Keep your money moving. Use your excess cash flow to create new positive situations. Add a new product or service, for example. Just remember to keep your cash flow positive with a reasonable margin of error.

Maintain profits and a positive cash flow and you will succeed unequivocally. You will never run out of money.

The higher your gross profit margin, the easier it is to make profits and maintain a positive cash flow. Gross margin is the difference between your selling price and the actual cost of manufacturing your product or providing your service (before deducting any other expenses). If your gross margin is only 10% it's harder to keep a positive cash flow than if your gross margin is 50%.

The lower your overhead (the actual costs of doing business such as rent, employees, phones, lights, heat, insurance, travel, shipping, equipment, etc.), the easier it is to maintain a positive cash flow.

If you follow the Entrepreneur's Four Basic Principles of Financial Success, you will become successful and independent:

1. Gather information to continually give your customers, employees, and suppliers what they need and want.

2. Keep your gross profit margins as high as possible.

3. Keep your overhead as low as possible.

4. Keep your cash flow positive. (The goal is to achieve profits and a positive cash flow as soon as possible and to keep it positive.)

What about those old American dream stories? You know, the immigrant who gets off the boat with no money in his pocket. Somehow, he starts buying shoelaces on credit for a penny, and selling them. Suddenly, ten years later, this guy's a multimillionaire.

Well, you can be absolutely sure about four things:

1. He had the information about where to buy and sell shoelaces.

2. He kept his gross margins high.

3. He kept his overhead low.

4. He maintained a positive cash flow.

The American dream *can* happen today—it's now more possible than ever. In fact, with the vast amount of information available today, opportunities are actually greater than ever before. The basic rules of the game haven't

The Entrepreneur's Principles of Financial Success

1. Gather Information To Continually Give Your Customers, Employees, And Suppliers What They Need And Want.

2. Keep Your Gross Profit Margins As High As Possible.

3. Keep Your Overhead Low.

4. Keep Your Cash Flow Positive. (The Goal Is To Achieve Profits And A Positive Cash Flow As Soon As Possible And To Keep It Positive.)

changed. Only the times have changed.

When I was eighteen years old, I started selling wigs out of the back of my car. The business was based on the fourth floor of an old office building and the rent was $55 per month. I had a pay phone on the wall instead of an office phone because it was cheaper. I received the information that the local beauty salons were purchasing the most popular wigs from distributors for $31 each and reselling them to their customers.

Then I saw an ad for wholesale wigs in the Sunday Business Opportunities section of *The New York Times* (I was living in Boston at the time). I called the telephone number listed in the ad and discovered that I could buy the same wigs in small quantities for $28 each, and in large quantities for $20 each.

Because my overhead was so low, I could afford to undercut the competition. So I started distributing and selling the wigs to beauty salons for $30 apiece (even though I was paying $28 each, which was less than a 10% gross margin). Because I undercut the competition by $1 per wig, I started selling lots of wigs and was soon able to buy them at $20 each with the volume discount. Then I made $10 on each wig, a 33% gross margin. Eventually we imported them directly from Hong Kong and soon thereafter became part owners of the wig factory that produced them. That business became a major success and eventually we sold it to an international conglomerate for millions of dollars when I was still very young. All of this resulted from using one piece of information from *The New York Times* to my benefit.

Remember: The less cash you have available, the more important it is to gather information and to plan in order to keep a positive cash flow. You can plan to work out of your house, keep your job, and sell shoelaces (or whatever you choose) at night until you build up enough sales volume to accumulate some cash and have enough steady income (positive cash flow) to support yourself and the overhead. Then you can quit your job and grow your business further.

As your sales and cash on hand (profits) build, you can rent an office or hire a salesperson. But your decisions must be numbers-guided and remain numbers-guided. That will never change. The only thing that changes is the scope of your planning.

Some people can't start small and keep their overhead low because their egos are too big. Especially people who might be used to working for large companies. Sometimes they feel that it's below their stature to work from a small office or forego a fancy company car. The principle is simple: High overhead never made anyone a success. But it has paid for a lot of failures.

Success will happen if you let the numbers guide you. Gather the optimal information, have patience, and persevere. There is no mystique about it.

Here are some tips you can use to build financial independence.

Know Your Numbers

Have all the financial information at your fingertips, your sales, accounts receivable, inventory, and accounts payable. Learn how they interrelate. Understand the basics of bookkeeping. Take a bookkeeping course. Learn how to do your own spread sheets and weekly, monthly, quarterly, and yearly cash flow analyses on a computer and do them.

Staying Power

Staying power means that if things go badly, you'll have enough cash to survive. Be conservative about your anticipated sales and expenses when you're preparing your business plan and spread sheets. Staying power is a key to success.

Collect Your Receivables

Collect all the money that's owed to you when it's owed to you. Unless you've been told up front that payment clearly would be slower than your stated terms, or unless extenuating circumstances exist, which is very rare, collect all the money that is owed to you when it's owed to you. If you did the work as agreed, you're entitled to get paid as agreed, on time. (The same rule applies to paying your suppliers.)

Just-in-Time Inventory Management

Always have the information about the exact inventory your customer needs and wants and have it just in time, when it's needed and wanted. This not only satisfies your customers, the reason you're in business, but it also insures that you won't have any excess inventory or work in process. The costs associated with excess inventory are no less a black hole than overhead, maybe more.

Use Money, Don't Spend It

Think about every penny you spend as an investment in building your business. There are only three reasons to spend money: to better satisfy your existing customers, to get new customers, and to add to your independence.

Your Customers Come First

The basic objective of business is to continually give the customer a great deal. You always want to lower the cost of your goods and/or service. And you always want to lower your overhead. But never sacrifice quality, service, or the satisfaction of your customers. Focus first on satisfying your customer and the money will come.

Proof Positive

Profit is proof you've done a good job gathering information, thinking about it, and using it to provide a product or service that pleases your customers. Profit is also your reward for being productive.

Don't Let the Tail Wag the Dog

Don't make business decisions based primarily on their tax consequences. The correct business decision is the first priority. It is much better to make a good business decision, make money, and pay the tax than it is to make a bad business decision solely to avoid paying tax. You may not pay any tax, but you won't make any money, either.

The Ultimate Decision

Always invest in your business for the future as you must, but always ask yourself if the money you're investing is consistent with your original idea of giving your customers what they need and want. Make all important financial decisions with all the information you can possibly have available. Will this decision make you more independent without seriously risking any independence you've already earned?

CHAPTER FOURTEEN

A Way of Thinking

Being an Entrepreneur Isn't a Job, It's a Way of Life

Thinking like an entrepreneur is a way of life, an attitude. It requires putting yourself in a state of perpetual growth and renewal by continuously gathering and thinking about new information to give to customers, employees, and suppliers. You give what all these people need and want and you get what you need and want in return. What could be more invigorating?

Being an entrepreneur is all about working hard and thinking hard in the information age. The entrepreneur's craft is making money with information and energy. You must have the information about management, marketing, and money. Find out more every day. It's the only way to stay ahead of the game.

Once you realize that constantly gathering, thinking about, and using information is the fuel for your business decisions, the key to keeping your customers, employees, and suppliers happy, and the source of your financial and personal independence, you will naturally carry on the process every waking hour. Time, as you knew it, will become meaningless.

Your mind has no punch clock. It doesn't turn on at nine and turn off at five. Even your family vacations will become refreshing times to gather and think about information. You

You are always thinking about the three fundamental areas of business—management, marketing, and money.

will always return home renewed and brimming with new ideas.

When I was vacationing in Florida, I visited a friend who was in business there. Across his office hallway was a huge suite of modern offices. On the door to the suite was the word "offices." There was no indication of the kind of offices. Curiosity got the best of me. I learned that these offices were shared by a variety of businesspeople. It was the first shared office complex I had ever encountered and I have used that information often in my own businesses and recommended it to others as well as an excellent and inexpensive way to get a business off the ground.

Information is limitless. There's always more of it and it's always changing. In order to keep up with it, you're going to eat it, breathe it, and sleep it. And always be thinking about how to gather more of it and how best to use it to gain experience and become knowledgeable.

Whatever business you choose to go into, expect some grueling and unpleasant times. Things always take twice as long and cost twice as much as you think they should. Because you can see your dreams so clearly, it's easy to minimize the length of time and amount of money that will be necessary to achieve them. But financial independence is the deep-rooted motivator and nothing is so encouraging as seeing your success on the horizon. Keep your eyes on your dream and you will soon love the process of thinking like, and being, an entrepreneur.

CHAPTER FIFTEEN

Choosing the Right Business

Is It the Right Time to Start?

Selecting the right business is a personal and challenging decision. Literally thousands of possibilities exist. You are choosing the vehicle that will carry you to personal independence.

Keep three extremely useful guidelines in mind as you go through this process of gathering information to make your decision: Love, Knowledge, and Positioning.

Since your business is an extension of yourself, determine what you love doing and where your interest and knowledge lie. Choose a business that can utilize these strengths. Maybe it's furniture, travel, fishing, knitting, computers, biology, physics, or astronomy. You will spend much time working and thinking about your business, make sure you choose an industry that you love.

For example, if you enjoy food and cooking, hundreds of opportunities are available in the food industry. You could open a restaurant, a catering service, or develop a software program for the food industry. You could start a pasta manufacturing company, publish recipe books, open a cooking school, or become a fancy food manufacturer. Remember to expand upon your interests and stay within an area that you enjoy.

In addition to a love of your chosen field, an entrepreneur should also have related hands-on experience in one of the three fundamental areas of business: marketing, management, and money. Perhaps you have experience as a bookkeeper or have worked in a bank (money), or have managed an office or run a summer camp (management), or have worked in manufacturing, advertising, or sales (marketing). This type of experience is valuable for entrepreneurs.

Of utmost importance when selecting a business to enter is positioning. You need to find what marketing people call a "niche" or a "hole in the market." That means you must have information about a need, want, or desire in the marketplace that isn't being satisfied.

If you are selling left-handed surgical instruments to doctors, you have a "niche" market. If you lived in a town with ten Chinese restaurants but no Italian restaurants, that could be your "hole" in the market.

Almost any business can make money with the right niche, or hole, in the market...if its positioning is correct. Provided all other important aspects are in place.

You want to become an entrepreneur in order to build your financial and personal independence. The time to start is right if you love what you've chosen, have some knowledge of it, have positioned it properly, and made a business plan to test and finance your idea.

Choose a business you love.

CHAPTER SIXTEEN

The Entrepreneur's Law of Eventual Success

Information + Persistence = Success

Success is getting everything you need and want by doing what you love to do.

Information is the basis of all success. Knowledge comes from information. Knowledge is information you can use. The amount of effort you put into gathering, thinking about, interpreting, and deciding on information about your business and giving your customers, employees, and suppliers what they need and want is directly related to your success. It's the strictest kind of cause and effect. You can only succeed by knowing what to do, and by doing it. And knowing what to do is totally information- and experience-based.

You have to build your own wealth of experience and knowledge by living the process of running your own business. Experience is based totally on fact; no speculation is involved. What happened, happened. You can enrich your experience and make it more valuable by thinking about it, dissecting it, and analyzing it to make sure that you learn the most from everything that happens. Good or bad.

The process of continually thinking about the information that caused a given effect is critical. What were the

Success is
Getting Everything You
Need And Want By
Doing What You
Love To Do.

consequences of each decision? What could I have done differently to create a better outcome? These are the questions whose answers will lead to knowledge. Knowledge from experience is the most powerful and best information you can have. Knowledge from experience is information that you fully understand, and that you can use and rely on.

Just use common sense and gain experience. The more experience you have about a particular topic, the easier it will be to think about and use new information relating to that topic (like in a connect-the-dots game, the more dots you've connected, the easier it is to know the outcome). Everything becomes easy once you know it.

And once you've gained knowledge from experience, it's yours—and always there to help you. Your accumulation of information, knowledge, and experience are the guarantors of your success.

Success is not a place. You don't reach it, you live it. Success is the ongoing process of making a string of correct decisions. Successful decisions are made by taking all available information, thinking about it, applying patience, and making a decision.

If your decision is a good one, think about it, learn from it, and add it to your information base. If it turns out to be a mistake, you'll learn from it as well and get it right the next time. Then you'll succeed. Mistakes are an inte-

The Entrepreneur's Law of Eventual Success.

gral part of success if you use them correctly...and don't make them twice.

Every mistake furnishes an opportunity to learn. Learn from every failure and every mistake. There's no better teacher than experience. There is actually no such thing as a pure mistake. There are positive and negative learning experiences. By learning what doesn't work you may find that you actually learn what does work too.

When you're starting out as an entrepreneur and gaining experience, the biggest surprise would be to have no surprises. Experience is gained from the practice of making decisions and from living with their consequences. As you gain more experience, you will also gain more respect for the information you have to work with. Your experience and knowledge will confirm that you will only be as successful as your information and experience and your ability to think about, interpret, and apply them.

You have to realize that collecting the information you need every day is in fact going after success every day and not waiting for success to come to you. You've got to enjoy the process and have the right attitude and thinking process to accompany this journey. Once you achieve that method of working and thinking, you will be a success.

I've been an entrepreneur for 27 years. I've built companies worth many millions of dollars each on five separate occasions. If I had adopted the mindset and had all the information and knowledge that's contained in this book when I started out, each of my successes would have equalled or surpassed all of my successes combined.

Remember the following rules of success throughout your entrepreneurial career:

1. Always seek new information to continue to give your customers, employees, and suppliers what they need and want. Learn how to use information to gain knowledge and make decisions. An entrepreneur uses information to create knowledge to make money and to replace the need for money.

2. Each and every action you take, each and every decision you make creates either a positive or negative situation. Strive to create positive situations. Be patient. Never react quickly to any situation that bothers you. If a situation bothers you, pause. Even if your pause lasts seven days, figure out how to turn that negative situation into a positive one. If a situation is positive, pause long enough to add humility. Real creativity lies in the ability to create positive situations for everyone: your customers, your employees, your suppliers, your community, and yourself.

3. The three fundamental legs of business are management, marketing, and money. You need constantly updated information and knowledge about all three. All three are totally interrelated and interdependent. Without all three legs fully standing, the stool will fall.

4. Learn to control your ego. Always keep focused on accomplishing your original idea of giving your customers what they need and want.

5. Persist and never doubt your ability to gather information, gain experience, and make successful decisions.

The Entrepreneur's Law of Eventual Success is: No matter how many mistakes you make, as long as you continue to devote yourself to learning from your mistakes and to correcting them quickly, to gathering information and experience about your customers, your employees, and your suppliers and to keeping them happy, and continue to persist you will build up a critical mass of experience and knowledge that will lead to eventual success.

If you follow the principles about information and knowledge as outlined in this book, you will succeed.

THE UNITED STATES OF
ONE DOLLAR

CHAPTER SEVENTEEN

CHARITY

The Responsibility of Success

Donating a certain percentage of your time and profits to charity is a responsibility. (Participating and giving also make you feel good.) Giving and sharing are constant reminders that the real purpose of making money is to create positive situations. Creating positive situations and helping others by sharing are powerful ways of saying thank you to the Universe for your success.

The decision to give is strictly personal, to be done quietly and not to be used primarily, if at all, for publicity. The most gracious way to give is in honor or in memory of another person.

The Entrepreneur's Checklists

What You Should Know Before You Start Your Business

1. I feel a strong desire for personal and financial independence.
2. I chose to start a business that I love.
3. I know my own strengths and weaknesses.
4. I fully understand that information is the key to business strength. I also fully understand how information relates to stress, luck, change, short- and long-term planning, money, and success.
5. I know where to find relevant information on a daily basis.
6. I have found a niche in the market.
7. I know my customers: I understand what they need and know how to provide it.
8. I realize that the three fundamental areas of business – Management, Marketing and Money, are all interrelated. And I know I must fully understand all three, or that I must have employees or a network of professionals and consultants who have had experience and knowledge of all three.
9. I have gathered all the information about my competition and I know that my product or service has a distinct advantage.
10. I have written a business plan.
11. I'm starting my business with as low an overhead as possible and I have enough capital to keep going if the business isn't as profitable as planned.
12. My product or service is correctly positioned in the marketplace. I have done everything possible so that my customers can't afford *not* to buy it.
13. I am prepared to continually "bonk" my ego for the sake of my customers', suppliers', employees', as well as my own success.
14. I understand the importance of admitting and correcting my mistakes quickly, of gaining experience, and of being persistent. I understand how these factors relate to my eventual success.
15. I fully understand the decision-making process. (See Chapter Four.)

What You Should Ask Yourself Every Day You Operate Your Business

1. Did I make every effort to collect new information today that relates to my business? Did I engage in networking?
2. Did I spend time thinking about and acting on the three fundamental areas of my business – Management, Marketing, and Money?
3. Did I remind myself to focus on my customer? Did I talk to at least one customer today, and did I listen carefully to learn if I could better serve my customer both today and in the future?
4. Did I check on what my competitors are doing?
5. Were all of my activities and actions consistent with my business plan? Were all my actions consistent with both my short- and long-term plans?
6. Did I review each decision to understand why they were successful or not? Do I know what I'd do differently?
7. Did I substitute information for money wherever possible?
8. Did I think about keeping my gross margins as high as possible, and keeping my overhead as low as possible?
9. Did I think about ways to increase my cash flow and profits?
10. Did I respectfully listen to my employees and suppliers with an open mind, and make changes for the better?
11. Did I try to create a win-win situation with every negotiation process?
12. Did I "bonk" my ego at least once today? Did I strive to create only positive situations?
13. Has each of my decisions made me more personally and financially independent?
14. Did I follow the decision-making process as closely as possible? (See Chapter Four.)
15. Did I think about giving either money or time to charity?

Notes

Notes

Notes